I Can't Quit

Your Guide to Holding on When Everything Is Falling Apart

by Paul Roberts
I Can't Quit Series Publishing

www.icantquitlife.com

© 2025 by Paul Dallas Roberts

All rights reserved. No part of this publication may be reproduced, distributed, or transmitted in any form or by any means, including photocopying, recording, or other electronic or mechanical methods, without the prior written permission of the publisher, except in the case of brief quotations embodied in critical reviews and certain other noncommercial uses permitted by copyright law.

Published by I Can't Quit Publishing
Dallas, Texas
Used by permission. All rights reserved worldwide.

ISBN: 979-8-9985494-2-7
Printed in the United States of America
Second Edition
Cover design by I Can't Quit Series Publishing
Published by I Can't Quit Series Publishing
www.ICantQuitLife.com

For more resources and upcoming books in the *I Can't Quit* Series, visit
www.ICantQuitLife.com

Dedication

I dedicate this book to YOU.

You matter. Your life matters. You didn't pick this book up by accident, you picked it up because something inside of you knows there's more. My prayer is that as you read, you'll find the strength to keep moving forward, no matter what you're facing.

To my mom—look, you're still changing lives. All because you had faith in me when I couldn't see anything worth saving in myself. Your belief carried me, and now that belief lives on in every person who chooses not to quit.

To Tamara and my kids, thank you for walking with me through the darkest days and for reminding me that love is stronger than failure. Every sober sunrise, every mile I run, and every page I write is because you kept believing I could.

To my recovery family—you showed me what real strength looks like. You proved to me that we don't get to the finish line alone. We carry each other.

And to every fighter, struggler, and dreamer who ever thought about giving up—this is your book.

Because here's the truth: what you will learn is that when you become successful, you'll realize it was never about you. You succeed so that someone else can succeed. You climb the mountain so you can reach down and pull the next person up.

Success doesn't belong to you. Success belongs to the people you help.

That's the real legacy.

Table of Contents

- Title Page
- Copyright
- Dedication
- Table of Contents
- Preface
- Introduction

Chapters

1. When Quitting Looks Easier
2. More in the Tank Than You Think (Frankl & Goggins)
3. Built to Endure
4. Activity Over Emotion
5. Keep Firing
6. Stop Talking. Start Doing
7. The Awesome Responsibility of Making Money
8. The Two-Year Window
9. Surround Yourself with Strength
10. One More Mile

- Conclusion: The Legacy of Not Quitting (The Four Pillars)
- The I Can't Quit Declaration
- For Real Estate Agents Who Can't Quit
- About the Author

PREFACE

If you read this book, and if you do the steps at the end of each chapter, you will quit quitting.

You will break the habit of giving up.
You will find grit inside you that you didn't know you had.

That's my guarantee.

This isn't a book about feeling better. It's a book about getting stronger. This is straight in your face… "you can't quit" — with stories, scars, and steps that will force you to move forward when everything in you wants to stop.

Think of it like a punch to the gut, a slap across the back of the head, a Godsmack right on your face. Because sometimes that's what we need — not another pep talk, but a jolt of reality.

Life is brutal. Business is brutal. Marriage, money, health — brutal. And when you're down in it, quitting looks like relief. I know, because I've been there. More times than I care to admit.

But quitting is a lie. Quitting doesn't make the pain stop — it just guarantees regret.

So, here's what you're holding:
- Raw stories of almost quitting.
- Truths from men who endured the unimaginable — Viktor Frankl in a concentration camp, David Goggins pounding through pain.
- My own scars are from repossessions, IRS battles, foreclosure, betrayal, addiction, and running until I couldn't

run anymore.
- **And, most important, action steps you can take when everything in you screams "quit."**

This book is short because you don't need more words. You need fire. You need focus. You need to remember that quitting is not an option.

So buckle up. These next pages aren't polished. They're survival.

INTRODUCTION

Life will pin you down.

The enemy — whether it's financial pressure, addiction, betrayal, or the thoughts in your own head — will close in. And in that moment, you don't rise in glory. You don't wave a white flag.

You do the one thing that gives you a chance to survive: you keep firing.

My grandfather fought in World War II, and I'll never forget the words he once told me about holding the line. I'll share more of his story later, but his lesson stuck with me: *don't stop firing.*

That's what this book is about.
Not perfection.
Not comfort.
Not an easy road.

It's about survival.
It's about refusing to quit when everything in you wants to.

Think of it like a Godsmack right to your face. Because sometimes that's what we need — not another pep talk, but a jolt of reality.

Life is brutal. Business is brutal. Marriage, money, health — brutal. And when you're down in it, quitting looks like relief. I know, because I've been there. More times than I care to admit.

But quitting is a lie. Quitting doesn't make the pain stop — it just guarantees regret.

So, here's what you're holding:

- Raw stories of almost quitting.
- Truths from men who endured the unimaginable — Viktor Frankl in a concentration camp, David Goggins pounding through pain.
- My own scars are from repossessions, IRS battles, foreclosure, betrayal, addiction, and running until I couldn't run anymore.
- And, most important, action steps you can take when everything in you screams "quit."

This book is short because you don't need more words. You need fire. You need to focus. You need to remember that quitting is not an option.

So, buckle up. These next pages aren't polished. They're survival.

So, buckle up. Keep your head down. Keep firing.

Let's go to war with quitting.

CHAPTER 1:

When Quitting Looks Easier

I've been there.

That moment when the weight feels unbearable, when every voice inside your head whispers the same word: *quit.*

For me, it wasn't just a bad day. It was a season of darkness. Business wasn't moving. Money was thin. Relationships were strained. Every step forward felt like dragging concrete shoes through quicksand. I'd wake up and wonder if all the sacrifice was worth it. I questioned myself, my abilities, even my calling.

And I'll be honest — quitting looked like relief.

It looked like finally getting the pressure off my back.
It looked like not having to fight another day.
It looked like peace.

But here's the truth I had to learn the hard way: quitting doesn't bring peace. Quitting multiplies the pain.

When you quit, you don't just stop the fight — you surrender the reward. You give up on the seeds you've already planted. You walk away from the people counting on you. And worse, you teach yourself that quitting is an option.

The day I almost walked away from the business, I told myself: *This isn't working. It's too hard. Maybe I'm not cut out for this.* I was tired of rejection, tired of bills piling up, tired of feeling like I was running in circles.

But as I sat in the middle of that storm, one thought cut through the noise:

What if tomorrow is the day everything changes? What if the breakthrough is closer than I think?

That single thought was enough to keep me moving. Not fast. Not perfect. Just moving.

And every single time I wanted to quit after that; I leaned on something else too: the people around me.

When I looked up and saw others in my circle succeeding — building, winning, growing — it gave me oxygen. It kept air in my lungs. I realized: if they can push through, so can I. If I'm around people who won't quit, then neither will I.

See, the lie of quitting is that it will ease the pain. But the truth is, it only guarantees regret. And regret weighs more than failure ever will.

So when you feel like quitting — and you will — pause long enough to ask yourself this: *What if I'm closer to the breakthrough than I realize?*

Hold on one more day. Make one more call. Take one more step.

Because quitting may look easier, but it never leads to freedom. Only pressing through does.

I almost quit. But I didn't.
And that one decision made all the difference.

TAKEAWAY

Quitting is a lie that looks like peace but delivers only regret.

ACTION STEP

Write down the area of your life right now where quitting feels easiest. Then ask yourself two questions:

1. *What reward, breakthrough, or person am I walking away from if I quit today?*
2. *Do I have people around me who are succeeding and encouraging me to keep going?*

If the answer to #2 is no, it's time to change your circle.

DAILY CHECK-IN

- Did you set and pursue a clear daily goal today?
- Did you read for 15 minutes this morning to stay mentally and spiritually fit?
- Did you read for 15 minutes tonight before bed to reset your focus?
- Did you get some form of exercise in today to stay physically fit?
- Did you take at least one step toward financial health or growth?

Remember: success isn't built in a day. It's built daily.

CHAPTER 2:

More in the Tank Than You Think

When I first read Viktor Frankl's *Man's Search for Meaning*, it broke me. To this day, when I pick it up, I feel my chest tighten and my eyes water. I still wonder how a man could endure such hell—and how other men could be so cruel.

Frankl was stripped of everything. Literally. Prisoners arriving at the camps were herded off the trains, ordered to undress, their hair shaved, their names erased. They were yelled at, spit on, and beaten. Humanity reduced to a number tattooed on the skin.

But the worst wasn't just the humiliation. It was the constant threat of death. If you showed weakness, if you limped, if you looked too sick to work—you were sent to the gas chamber. It didn't matter if you were broken inside. You had to endure, to act strong, to hide your pain, or you'd be marked for death.

And here's the cruelest twist: sometimes the ones doing the yelling, the hitting, the choosing—were your own people. Jewish prisoners called capos were given small privileges if they agreed to keep order, but in the end, most of them met the same fate in the gas chamber. It was a sick, twisted world where cruelty was currency.

Reading Frankl's words, I've often thought: if they could endure that—surely, I can endure this. Surely, we all can. Because there has never been suffering in human history so systematic, so dehumanizing, so unthinkable—and yet, many still lived, still chose to fight for meaning.

Frankl discovered something that can't be stripped away: the freedom to choose your response. Even in a concentration camp, he said, man can decide whether to give up or to hold onto meaning. And those who found meaning—whether in the thought of reuniting with family, finishing a piece of work, or simply proving that the human spirit could outlast horror—were the ones who endured.

That's when it hit me: the limit isn't what happens to you. The limit is what you decide what it means.

And then—thousands of miles and decades away—David Goggins said the same thing, in his own brutal way.

Goggins, a Navy SEAL and ultra-runner, built his life around finding out what's left after your body says you're done. He calls it the **40% Rule**:

> "When you think you're done, you're only 40% into what your body can do. That's just the limits we put on ourselves." (*Can't Hurt Me*)

Think about that. The wall you hit—the "I can't go any further" moment—isn't the end. It's not even halfway. There's still 60% left in the tank.

And just like Frankl's lesson, it's not about comfort. It's about meaning. It's about deciding: *this pain isn't the end, it's the beginning of who I really am.*

So, here's what I want you to see:
- Frankl proved endurance is spiritual. You can live through the unthinkable if you hold onto meaning.
- Goggins proved that endurance is physical. You can push past the wall if you refuse to believe the lie that you're done.

Between the two, the message is clear:

You've got more in the tank than you think.

TAKEAWAY

Your limits are not your end. They are the beginning of your true capacity.

ACTION STEP

The next time you feel like quitting, pause and ask yourself two questions:

1. *What meaning can I hold onto right now that makes this pain worth it?* (Frankl)
2. *If I'm only at 40%, what's one more step I can take today?* (Goggins)

Write it down. Then do it.

DAILY CHECK-IN

- Did you set and pursue a clear daily goal today?
- Did you read for 15 minutes this morning to stay mentally and spiritually fit?
- Did you read for 15 minutes tonight before bed to reset your focus?
- Did you get some form of exercise in today to stay physically fit?
- Did you take at least one step toward financial health or growth?

Remember: success isn't built in a day. It's built daily.

CHAPTER 3:

Build to Endure

If you ever need a cure for self-pity, pick up Viktor Frankl's *Man's Search for Meaning*.

I can promise you — whatever you're going through, whatever feels unbearable — it will reframe everything.

Frankl lived through one of the ugliest, most dehumanizing experiences in human history: the Nazi concentration camps. Everything was stripped away — clothes, dignity, identity, family. They were treated like animals, shaved and numbered, shoved into freezing barracks, starved until bones poked through skin.

But here's what broke me when I read his book: even in that nightmare, some prisoners chose to endure with dignity.

Frankl wrote about how men would march out to work in the cold, exhausted and starving, yet some of them would quietly hum songs. Others would share their last crust of bread with someone weaker than themselves. And every now and then, someone would pause, point out a sunset beyond the barbed wire, and whisper about its beauty — as if the soul could rise above the barbed wire for just a moment.

Think about that. When everything in their lives was taken away, when death hung over them daily, they still found ways to sing, to give, to notice beauty.

That's not weakness. That's strength at its purest.

Frankl discovered a truth that's easy to forget when life feels like it's falling apart: **we are built to endure.**

He realized that suffering, no matter how deep, becomes bearable when it has meaning. And meaning can be found in the smallest, most ordinary things — in love, memory, in service, in faith. It's not about escaping pain. It's about finding something larger than the pain to hold onto.

So, when you feel like giving up — when you're ready to throw yourself a pity party because life isn't fair — remember this: people once sang on the way to slave labor in the snow, with death camps behind them and no guarantee of survival ahead.

If they could endure that, then surely you can endure this.

TAKEAWAY

Endurance is not about avoiding suffering. It's about rising above it with meaning.

ACTION STEP

Practicing Endurance

Endurance is not just an idea — it's something you can strengthen. Here's a simple exercise to remind yourself that even in pain, beauty still exists:

1. **Get still.** Find a quiet moment with a notebook or a piece of paper.

2. **Write it down.** List three things in your life that still hold beauty, even in the middle of hardship. These could be people you love, memories that give you hope, or simple daily gifts like sunlight through the window.

3. **Keep it close.** Place that list somewhere you'll see it often — in your journal, your phone, or even on your bathroom mirror.

4. **Return to it.** Whenever you feel crushed, read it aloud and remind yourself:
"I am built to endure."

DAILY CHECK-IN

- Did you set and pursue a clear daily goal today?
- Did you read for 15 minutes this morning to stay mentally and spiritually fit?
- Did you read for 15 minutes tonight before bed to reset your focus?
- Did you get some form of exercise in today to stay physically fit?
- Did you take at least one step toward financial health or growth?

Remember: success isn't built in a day. It's built daily.

CHAPTER 4:

Activity Over Emotion

I've learned something the hard way: emotions will lie to you. Activity never does.

When everything was falling apart — cars repossessed, IRS breathing down my neck, saying goodbye to a house I thought we'd live in forever — the pain should have crushed me. But it didn't. Do you know why? Because I stayed in motion.

We packed in the middle of the night so no one would know. We loaded boxes in the dark, slipping out quietly because I didn't want my team to see us losing it all. I didn't want the confusion, the questions, the fear. So, I kept moving.

And I'll be honest — for a moment, I started to feel sorry for myself. That house was where I got sober. Walking out of it hurt. But then, in the middle of the sadness, something shifted. I thought: *Wait. My next house will be the one where I'm always sober. A house with new memories. A house with no blackouts. A house with no stupid, drunken fights with Tamara.*

That thought gave me power. It gave me vision. And vision pulled me forward.

That's when it hit me: activity cures pain. Motion kills despair.

Most people make the mistake of sitting in their suffering. They talk about it. They rehearse it. They polish it like a speech. And the more they repeat it, the deeper it digs into their identity.

But here's the truth: pain doesn't get smaller when you talk about it. Pain gets smaller when you outrun it.

I can't tell you how many people I've met who stop me after I speak and say, "I'm going through the exact same thing." And I listen, I hug them, I care for them. But inside, I'm screaming: *Stop telling the story until you have a victory to go with it.*

Because the story of pain without the story of victory is just a sad song you keep on repeat.

Listen to me: the only thing that separates the people who drown from the people who climb out is this — **they kept moving.**

I didn't escape pain when I walked away from 627 Santa Fe. I didn't escape stress when I moved into a rental. I didn't escape fear when the bills piled up. But I refused to freeze. I made calls. I stayed active. I pictured the future instead of rehearsing the past.

That's why I made it through.

TAKEAWAY

You can't out-think despair. You can only outwork it. Activity cures everything.

ACTION STEP

The Motion List

1. Take out a piece of paper and write down **five simple actions** you can do today that require movement — a walk around the block, cleaning your desk, sending a thank-you text, organizing one drawer, making one call.

2. Don't rank them, don't overthink them — just list them.

3. Pick one and do it right now.

4. When you're done, cross it off and feel the small win. Activity builds on itself.

DAILY CHECK-IN

- Did you set and pursue a clear daily goal today?
- Did you read for 15 minutes this morning to stay mentally and spiritually fit?
- Did you read for 15 minutes tonight before bed to reset your focus?
- Did you get some form of exercise in today to stay physically fit?
- Did you take at least one step toward financial health or growth?

Remember: success isn't built in a day. It's built daily.

CHAPTER 5:

Keep Firing

My grandfather fought in World War II.

He wasn't a commander. He wasn't decorated. He was just a kid — eighteen years old, drafted into the U.S. Army, and thrown onto the front lines with the 3rd Infantry Division. He didn't ask to be there. He didn't want to be there. But war doesn't give you choices.

He once told me about a moment when the enemy was pressing close. Bullets flying, shells exploding, men hitting the ground all around him. And in the middle of that chaos, his sergeant screamed:

"Keep your asses down and keep firing! Don't stop firing!"

That was the order. Stay low. Stay alive. Don't look up. Don't stop.

The men knew the truth — if you looked up, your head was gone. If you freeze, you were finished. If you quit firing, you were dead. The only hope was to keep pulling the trigger.

And that moment has lived in me ever since. Because that's not just war — that's life.

The Wounds He Carried

Eventually, my grandfather was hit. Shrapnel ripped through his body — arms, shoulders, stomach, legs. He should have died right there in the mud. Instead, he was flown to North Africa and put in a full body cast.

The records weren't clear — some say he was in that case six months, others nine. His letters home was censored, so no one really knew how bad it was. But what we do know is this: he had broken in body, but he refused to quit.

Nine months in a body cast. Nine months of immobility, pain, uncertainty. And still, he endured.

He came home scared of life, but alive. And he gave me a gift I didn't understand much later: the example of what it means to *keep firing* when everything in you wants to quit.

The Lesson in the Trenches

Sun Tzu once wrote that sometimes the wise move in battle is to retreat, to regroup, to wait for better ground. And there are times in life when that's true. But there are also moments when retreat is not an option.

Moments when the enemy is too close.
Moments when you're pinned down.
Moments when all you can do is keep your head down and keep firing.

Life will hand you trench moments.
Moments where you feel overwhelmed, surrounded, and hopeless.
Moments where quitting looks easier than pulling the trigger one more time.

That's when my grandfather's words echo in my head: *Don't stop firing.*

And here's the truth — most of the time, the enemy isn't even out there. It's here. In your head. The thoughts, the lies, the whispers telling you to quit.

When that enemy comes, you don't negotiate with it. You don't wait for it to back down. You fire back with activity. With discipline. With focus. With faith.

Because if you stop firing, you lose.

TAKEAWAY

Life will pin you down. The only way to survive is to keep your head down and keep firing.

ACTION STEP

Fire Back

1. Take a moment and **write down one battle in your life** where you feel pinned down right now.

2. Underneath it, list **three practical "shots" you can fire back this week** — small, specific actions that push you forward.
   (Example: make a call, finish a task, have a conversation, set a boundary.)

3. Commit to doing all three, no matter what. Each shot is proof you refuse to quit.

DAILY CHECK-IN

- Did you set and pursue a clear daily goal today?
- Did you read for 15 minutes this morning to stay mentally and spiritually fit?
- Did you read for 15 minutes tonight before bed to reset your focus?
- Did you get some form of exercise in today to stay physically fit?
- Did you take at least one step toward financial health or growth?

Remember: success isn't built in a day. It's built daily.

CHAPTER 6:

Stop Talking. Start Doing

I've heard a lot of stories.

After I speak on stage, people come up to me and pour their hearts out. They tell me about the cars they lost, the money they don't have, the relationships falling apart. And I care about them. I hug them. I listen.

But inside, I'm thinking: *Where's the victory?*

Because here's the hard truth: too many people rehearse their pain like it's a script. They know every line. They feel every tear. They can perform it on command. And the more they tell it, the deeper it carves into their identity.

But a story of pain without a story of victory is just victimhood on repeat.

Listen to me: I'm not saying don't talk to someone. I'm not saying you shouldn't share your struggles with a counselor, a trusted friend, or a mentor. What I'm saying is this — don't turn your scars into your stage show. Don't make your identity the story of your suffering.

The people who move forward are the ones who stop talking about what went wrong and start *doing* something to make it right.

When my house was gone, when my cars were repossessed, when the IRS was breathing down my neck — I didn't walk around telling everyone my sad story. I went to work. I pictured a new house. I made calls. I moved forward.

That's the difference.

Stop talking. Start doing.

Because activity is the only bridge from victim to victor.

TAKEAWAY

Your story isn't finished until you add the victory.

ACTION STEP

Rewrite the Story

1. Grab a notebook or piece of paper. **Write down the story you've been rehearsing** — the one you keep telling about why you're stuck. Be honest and unfiltered.

2. Now, underneath it, write **one practical step you can take this week** to begin changing that story. Make it small but specific.

3. Do it — and as you act, remind yourself: *this is how my story shifts from victim to victor.*

DAILY CHECK-IN

- Did you set and pursue a clear daily goal today?
- Did you read for 15 minutes this morning to stay mentally and spiritually fit?
- Did you read for 15 minutes tonight before bed to reset your focus?
- Did you get some form of exercise in today to stay physically fit?
- Did you take at least one step toward financial health or growth?

Remember: success isn't built in a day. It's built daily.

CHAPTER 7:

The Awesome Responsibility of Making Money

Pain has a purpose.

Every betrayal, every setback, every repossession, every "goodbye" to something you loved — it wasn't punishment. It was preparation.

Making a bunch of money is an awesome responsibility. And the truth is, most people aren't ready for it. That's why the pain comes first. It shapes you, humbles you, and prepares you to carry the weight.

I can promise you this with zero hesitation: it is easier to go from the bottom to the top than it is to go from the top to the bottom and somehow make it back again. Almost impossible.

That's why the pain you're in right now matters.

If you're crying out, wondering why it hurts so bad, wondering why you can't seem to get ahead — it's because there are lessons you haven't learned yet. Lessons you need before you're ready to carry the responsibility of wealth.

Because here's the truth: wealth without preparation will crush you.

The Curse of Sudden Wealth

Look at lottery winners. The statistics are brutal — within 18 months, most are right back where they started. Millions gone. Why? Because they weren't ready for the responsibility.

Look at Mike Tyson. One of the most feared fighters in history. In his prime, he made **$25 million in a single night**. One night. And yet he went broke. Why? Because he wasn't prepared for the awesome responsibility that comes with money.

Sudden wealth doesn't fix your problems. It amplifies them.

Even Guns N' Roses sang about it: the idea that stumbling onto a million dollars doesn't make life better — it makes it worse if you're not ready for it.

Money is a magnifier. If you're broken, it magnifies the brokenness. If you're undisciplined, it magnifies the chaos.

That's why God, in His mercy, doesn't hand you the money too soon. He knows it would destroy you.

Thank God for the Pain

So if you're broke right now, if you're struggling, if you're suffocating under the weight of your circumstances — thank God.

Seriously. Thank Him.

Because the pain you're in is proof that He's not done preparing you. He's shaping you, chiseling you, toughening you up for the responsibility that comes with wealth.

And when it comes — if you've learned the lessons — you'll be ready to carry it, not crushed by it.

TAKEAWAY

Pain isn't punishment. It's preparation. Making money is an awesome responsibility, and the suffering you're enduring right now is training you to carry it.

ACTION STEP

Preparation in Pain

1. Take a notebook and **list the three hardest things you're going through right now.**

2. Next to each one, write down the **lesson it's teaching you** — discipline, patience, humility, focus, or whatever it may be.

3. Under each struggle, write this sentence in your own handwriting:
   "This pain is preparing me for the responsibility I asked for."

4. Keep that page where you can see it. Every time the weight feels heavy, remind yourself: the pain has a purpose.

DAILY CHECK-IN

- Did you set and pursue a clear daily goal today?
- Did you read for 15 minutes this morning to stay mentally and spiritually fit?
- Did you read for 15 minutes tonight before bed to reset your focus?
- Did you get some form of exercise in today to stay physically fit?
- Did you take at least one step toward financial health or growth?

Remember: success isn't built in a day. It's built daily.

CHAPTER 8:

The Two-Year Window

Here's one of the hardest truths you'll ever swallow: most people quit right before it gets good.

They grind for a few months. They fight for a year. But when the results don't show up as fast as they hoped, they walk away.

And that's why most people never see their breakthrough.

I call it the **two-year window.**

Every great business, every great comeback, every great turnaround I've seen takes about two years of relentless consistency before the results start compounding. But the problem is, most people don't make it to the two-year mark. They get to 18 months, feel exhausted, and give up just before everything starts to click.

My Own Lesson

I've been there. I've been the guy staring at the bills, staring at the empty bank account, wondering if all the activity is even working. And the temptation to walk away was real.

But I learned something: the only way you lose is if you quit too soon.

Two years of activity — talking to people, making calls, building the systems, doing the unglamorous work — that's the runway.

That's when the snowball starts rolling. That's when the momentum builds. That's when the little wins finally explode into something you can't stop.

But you'll never see it if you quit at 18 months.

Why Two Years Matters

Think about it. Two years isn't forever. But it's long enough to:

- Outlast the people who were never serious in the first place.
- Build habits that no longer depend on motivation.
- See results that can't be faked, bought, or shortcut.

And here's the kicker: once you hit that window, the compounding takes over. What was once uphill starts to feel downhill.

But you'll never feel that if you quit too soon.

Stop Thinking Short-Term

We live in a microwave culture. Everybody wants success in thirty seconds or less. But life doesn't work that way. Wealth doesn't work that way. Legacy doesn't work that way.

It takes time. It takes repetition. It takes showing up when you don't want to.

The question is simple: are you willing to give yourself two years?

Because if you are, I promise you'll look back and realize the only thing standing between you and everything you wanted was the ability to outlast everyone else.

TAKEAWAY

The breakthrough always takes longer than you want, but quitting before the two-year mark guarantees you'll never see it.

ACTION STEP

Breakthrough Day

1. Identify **one area of your life or business** where you've been inconsistent — the place where quitting has been tempting.

2. On paper, write this commitment:
   "For the next two years, I will not quit on this no matter what."

3. Open your calendar and **circle the date two years from today.** Label it *Breakthrough Day*.

4. Every time you feel like quitting, look at that date and remind yourself: the breakthrough is coming if I don't stop.

DAILY CHECK-IN

- Did you set and pursue a clear daily goal today?
- Did you read for 15 minutes this morning to stay mentally and spiritually fit?
- Did you read for 15 minutes tonight before bed to reset your focus?
- Did you get some form of exercise in today to stay physically fit?
- Did you take at least one step toward financial health or growth?

Remember: success isn't built in a day. It's built daily.

CHAPTER 9:

Surround Yourself with Strength

Every time I wanted to quit, one thing kept me in a fight: the people around me.

When I looked up and saw others in my circle succeeding — building, growing, refusing to stop — it gave me oxygen. It kept air in my lungs when I felt like I couldn't breathe.

That's the power of community. The right people don't just inspire you. They sustain you.

Oxygen or Poison

The truth is, the people around you are either oxygen or poison.

- Oxygen people breathe life into your fight. They remind you of who you are when you forget. They hold you accountable when you want to run. They push you to go one more round when you've got nothing left.
- Poison people suck the strength right out of you. They complain. They gossip. They quit — and then try to convince you to quit with them.

Here's the hard reality: if your circle is filled with poison, you don't stand a chance. You will quit.

Everyone Has a Story, But No One Should Walk Alone

That's why I say: everyone has a story, but no one should walk alone.

I don't care how strong you think you are. I don't care how much discipline you've built. Nobody wins this fight in isolation.

You need people in your corner. People who will celebrate your wins but also call you out on your excuses. People who will tell you the truth when you'd rather hear a lie.

Because when you surround yourself with strength, you become strong.

Building Your Circle

So how do you do it?

- **Find people who are going where you want to go.** If you're the strongest one in your circle, you're in the wrong circle.
- **Cut ties with poison.** That doesn't mean I hate them. It means stopping giving them influence over your life.
- **Be the strength you want around you.** The fastest way to attract strong people is to become one yourself.

TAKEAWAY

Your circle will either suffocate you or sustain you. Choose oxygen.

ACTION STEP

Oxygen Check

1. Take out a sheet of paper and **list the five people you spend the most time with.**

2. Next to each name, write either **"Oxygen"** (they fuel you) or **"Poison"** (they drain you). Be brutally honest.

3. Choose **one intentional move this week** to spend more time with an oxygen person and less time with a poison person.

4. At the end of the week, reflect: did that choice give you more energy or less? Keep repeating it.

DAILY CHECK-IN

- Did you set and pursue a clear daily goal today?
- Did you read for 15 minutes this morning to stay mentally and spiritually fit?
- Did you read for 15 minutes tonight before bed to reset your focus?
- Did you get some form of exercise in today to stay physically fit?
- Did you take at least one step toward financial health or growth?

Remember: success isn't built in a day. It's built daily.

CHAPTER 10:

One More Mile

Sometimes survival is as simple as this: go one more mile.

When I run long distances, there's always a moment where my body screams, "Stop." My legs feel heavy, my lungs burn, my mind begs for relief. And every time, I remind myself: *Just go one more mile.*

Because one more mile changes everything.

One more mile gives you a different view.
One more mile proves your body can handle more than your mind told you it could.
One more mile turns weakness into strength, fear into faith, despair into momentum.

The Power of One More

Life works the same way.

When you feel like quitting your marriage, your business, your sobriety, your dreams — don't make a forever decision in a temporary moment. Just go one more mile.

Make one more call.
Have one more conversation.

Take one more step.

Because one more mile might be the mile where the breakthrough happens.

I Can't Quit Moments

History is full of people who refused to quit:

- Viktor Frankl — enduring unspeakable suffering in the camps yet choosing meaning over despair.
- David Goggins — running on broken legs, proving the 40% rule is real.
- My grandfather — bleeding in a trench, told to "keep firing," and doing exactly that.
- And me — repossessed cars, lost house, IRS breathing down my neck, but refusing to stop moving, building, and running forward.

Different stories. Same truth. They didn't quit. And neither can you.

Your Story Isn't Finished

I don't know what your "mile" looks like. Maybe it's staying sober one more day. Maybe it's making one more call when your business feels dead. Maybe it's walking back into your house tonight and choosing to love instead of leaving.

But I do know this: your story isn't finished if you don't stop.

Don't quit. Not today. Not tomorrow. Not ever.

TAKEAWAY

The breakthrough you're waiting for is always one more mile down the road.

ACTION STEP

Your One More Mile

1. Take a notebook and **write down the "mile" you're committing to this week** — the one action, step, or decision you'll make no matter what.

2. Be specific. *(Example: one more workout, one more sales call, one more day sober, one more conversation.)*

3. Put it somewhere visible — on your desk, your mirror, or your phone screen.

4. When the urge to quit shows up, look at that reminder and tell yourself: *Just one more mile.* Then do it.

DAILY CHECK-IN

- Did you set and pursue a clear daily goal today?
- Did you read for 15 minutes this morning to stay mentally and spiritually fit?
- Did you read for 15 minutes tonight before bed to reset your focus?
- Did you get some form of exercise in today to stay physically fit?
- Did you take at least one step toward financial health or growth?

Remember: success isn't built in a day. It's built daily.

CONCLUSION:
The Legacy of Not Quitting

It's normal to want to quit. It's normal to feel broken. But you don't have to give in.

Everything in this book — every story, every scar, every lesson — comes down to four pillars that carried me through:

- *Physically fit* — your body can endure more than you think.
- *Mentally fit* — discipline beats emotion every time.
- *Spiritually fit* — faith gives meaning to suffering.
- *Financially fit* — money is an awesome responsibility you must be prepared to carry.

If one of these pillars breaks, the others suffer. But when you strengthen all four, you become unshakable.

So don't quit. Not physically. Not mentally. Not spiritually. Not financially.

Too many people are waiting on your breakthrough. And your legacy begins the moment you refuse to quit.

THE I CAN'T QUIT DECLARATION

I declare today that I will not quit.
I may stumble. I may fall.
I may feel broken and weak.
But I will not quit.
My story isn't over — it's just beginning.

Signed: _____

FOR REAL ESTATE AGENTS WHO CAN'T QUIT

If you made it this far, you already know this: I don't quit.

And if you're a real estate agent who's tired of being stuck, tired of chasing the next deal, or tired of wondering if this business will ever truly give back to you — I built something for you.

It's called the **I Can't Quit 12-Week Coaching Program.**

Inside this program, I'll teach you how to:

- Build a business that actually lasts.
- Focus on the income-producing activities that create results.
- Surround yourself with a team that won't let you quit.

This isn't theory. It's a system that works. It's the same framework that's helped me build and scale businesses, survive rock bottom, and keep moving forward when everything in me wanted to stop.

If you're ready for more than just survival — if you're ready to thrive — then let's talk.

Because I won't quit on you.

☐ **Text me directly at 214-608-4307**
☐ Or visit **www.icantquitlife.com** to get started

Made in the USA
Coppell, TX
15 December 2025

65853554R00039